Best 100 Smoothies for Kids

Best 100 Smoothies for Kids

Incredibly Nutritious & Totally Delicious No-Sugar-Added Smoothies for Any Time of Day

Deborah Harroun

THE HARVARD COMMON PRESS · BOSTON, MASSACHUSETTS

The Harvard Common Press
www.harvardcommonpress.com

Printed in China
Printed on acid-free paper

Library of Congress Cataloging-in-Publication Data
Harroun, Deborah.
    Best 100 smoothies for kids : incredibly nutritious and totally delicious no-sugar-added smoothies for any time of day / Deborah Harroun.
        pages cm
    ISBN 978-1-55832-847-1 (paperback)
    1. Smoothies (Beverages) 2. Sugar-free diet--Recipes.
I. Title. II. Title: Best one hundred smoothies for kids.
    TX817.S636H37 2015
    641.8'75--dc23
                    2014041183

Front cover and interior photographs by Deborah Harroun

10 9 8 7 6 5 4 3 2 1

For **Abigail,**

Easton,

and Camden,

my favorite taste testers

Contents

Introduction

I always thought my kids would be the best eaters. In my dreams I would make curries and enchiladas and spinach quiche, and my kids would just gobble them up—and then ask for more. And at snacktime they'd beg for broccoli and carrot sticks.

Wow—did I have a rude awakening.

To give them credit, my kids actually ate quite well as babies. Each one of them was excited when I started to give them spoonfuls of sweet potato puree and mashed peas and carrots; they ate them with gusto. But once I made the switch from purees to regular solid food, things changed.

Today my kids have very different palates. Every day there's a new something that one of them won't eat. I started to worry about how many vitamins, minerals, and nutrients my kids were getting on a daily basis—especially since fresh fruits, and especially fresh vegetables, weren't at the top of the list of things they loved.

My kids wake up hungry, so mornings can be pretty crazy around my house. One morning I fed the kids breakfast and then made a smoothie for myself. They were there, watching me, and they all wanted to help Mom drink her smoothie.

That's when it hit me. Smoothies may be my answer to supplementing their diets with healthy foods. I would puree fruits and vegetables, adding protein and carbohydrates to their diet that would help them get through the day.

I started trying out different flavor combinations, and I was so happy to see how excited my kids were to drink smoothies. Even if they didn't end up liking some of the combinations I made, they would at least try them, which was a miracle in and of itself. And it turned out that my pickiest eater was actually the biggest smoothie fan.

While I still try to make sure there are fruits and vegetables on their plates at every meal, serving up a smoothie has helped to put my mind at ease. I know there is always at least one way to get my kids to try to eat healthy!

The Anatomy of a Smoothie

Once I discovered just how much my kids loved smoothies, I set out to find some great recipes. I was surprised, though, to find what kinds of ingredients went into many smoothie recipes that I came across. There were so many recipes that made huge smoothies filled with hundreds of empty calories as well as ingredients that were not necessarily healthy—like ice cream and lots of added sugar. I wanted to make sure that I was giving my children something healthy but also teaching them healthy eating habits. So there are a few things that set my smoothie recipes apart from many others.

First, there are *no added processed sugars*. All of the sugars in this book are natural, such as naturally sweet fruit. If I call for fruit juice, I advise readers to make sure they use 100 percent fruit juice with no added sugar. If a recipe needs a sweetener, I use the least possible amount of a natural sweetener such as agave syrup or honey. I do add sugar-free cookies to a few indulgent recipes; you should serve them sparingly, as a treat or dessert.

While I don't worry as much about calories for children since their growing brains and bodies require a healthy dose of calories, the serving sizes in these recipes are smaller and perfect for kids. Each serving is between 6 and 10 ounces. Kids will get plenty of nutrients, but they aren't having a whole day's worth of calories in one smoothie.

I've divided the smoothie recipes in this book into five chapters. You will find breakfast smoothies, lunchtime smoothies, snacktime smoothies, dessert smoothies, and bedtime smoothies. The **breakfast** chapter is full of recipes that will get your kids started off on the right foot for the day. They're filled with ingredients that taste great first thing in the morning, and they're packed with fiber and protein to help get your kids through the morning. The **lunchtime** smoothies are a little heartier, with ingredients that will help fill up little bellies. They are also a great way to give your kids a natural burst of energy that will keep them going through the afternoon. **Snacktime** smoothies are perfect for after school or as an afternoon snack when the kids start complaining that they're hungry, but it's not quite dinnertime yet. These smoothies will take the edge off their hunger without ruining their appetites when suppertime comes. The **dessert** smoothies are a bit more indulgent but are still filled with nutrients. I love giving my kids something healthy for dessert! All of the **bedtime** smoothies have secret ingredients—like cherries, which help regulate sleep cycles, and chamomile tea, which is calming—to help make sure your kids have the best night's sleep.

The Taste Testers

Every single smoothie in this book was taste tested by my three kids. Now, I won't exaggerate and say that every smoothie was a hit with all three, but I considered it a success if two of the three loved it. (It's impossible to please all of them every time!)

Abbi: My oldest (five at the time of the writing of this book) is an okay eater. She ate well as a baby, but at around two years old, she started to become very picky. As she has gotten older, she has become a lot better about trying new things, and actually liking new things. I can always get her to at least try a bite of everything on her plate, even if she doesn't end up wanting to eat it. Surprisingly, her favorites are shrimp and steak. And strawberries. You can't forget the strawberries!

Abbi is my biggest smoothie critic, though. She loves any smoothie with strawberries, but she doesn't like a lot of texture or seeds in her smoothies. And she does not like peppermint, so any smoothie with peppermint extract won't go over well with her.

Easton: My middle child, age three, is by far the pickiest. He thinks there should be only one food group—chocolate. He doesn't complain about not liking foods; he just won't eat something if he doesn't want it. He is the one I struggle with the most when it comes to eating quality food. His favorites are pasta, mom's homemade pizza, and bread. And did I mention chocolate?

Easton is the one who needs the smoothies most of all, because of his refusal to eat just about everything else. Luckily, he is a big smoothie fan. He will gladly take Abbi's serving of the mint-flavored smoothies. And while he is a chocoholic, he will drink any smoothie that is full of fruits or vegetables—including the green ones!

Camden: My youngest, age one, is my dream eater. Put anything in front of him, and he will devour it. I remember one night at the dinner table when he ate more than I did! I'm hoping his love of all kinds of food continues as he gets older. He doesn't care as much about raw vegetables, but if they are cooked, he will eat them. It's hard to define his favorites because he will eat anything!

Camden doesn't discriminate when it comes to smoothies. He will devour pretty much any flavor of smoothie, except for grapefruit.

The Equipment

All you really need for making smoothies is a blender. And while I believe that a high-speed blender like a Blendtec or Vitamix makes preparing smoothies easier, you don't have to shell out the big bucks in order to make smoothies at home. In fact, I tested every smoothie in this book with a lower-end blender, just to make sure that everyone can make each recipe at home. But here are a few things to keep in mind if you are not using a high-speed blender:

Without a high-speed blender, you may not get a super smooth consistency. Things like dates or oatmeal may not blend as well in a cheaper blender. You may end up with little chunks, so depending on your kids and their preferences, this might be an issue. Abbi does not like chunks or textures, so if I'm using a cheaper blender, I tend to skip recipes that use dates if I'm making a smoothie for her. Otherwise, I suggest soaking dates or oatmeal for 10 to 15 minutes. To get the smoothest consistency, blend the dates or oatmeal with the liquid called for in the smoothie before adding the rest of the ingredients.

You need less liquid in a high-speed blender. If you are using a high-speed blender, you might want to start with less liquid. When I used cheaper blenders, I noticed that more liquid was needed to keep the ingredients moving, because cheap blenders don't have as much power as the higher end machines. You may want to experiment by adding only part of the liquids to begin with, and then adding a bit at a time until you get the right consistency.

The order of ingredients doesn't matter as much in a high-speed blender. If you're using a high-speed blender, just throw the ingredients in and blend. If you are using a cheaper blender, start by adding the liquid, followed by frozen fruits and/or vegetables, then any additions, then any fresh fruits or vegetables. Add the ice last.

Be patient with a cheaper blender. You can make any smoothie in a cheaper blender, but you may have to stop several times to stir the ingredients around to get everything blended in. Just have patience and know that it may take several minutes.

In my opinion, there are a couple of other things that you need if you are serving smoothies to kids.

STRAWS

Even as an adult, I think it's sometimes hard to drink a smoothie—especially a thick one—straight from the glass. So unless I want to be cleaning smoothie mess off of my kids and my floor, I always keep straws on hand.

CUPS

I found that designated smoothie cups—ones with lids and straws that I could wash easily—were indispensable. Lids are important because many of the smoothies contain ingredients that will stain or make a mess, and, as you know, kids can get messy. Go for a simple design. The first cups I bought had straws that wound through different parts of the cup. It was practically impossible to get them clean. Colored cups are helpful if you have a child who is picky about the color of the smoothies. Green smoothies can be hidden away easily inside an opaque purple cup with a lid! But you might want some clear cups too for when you make a layered smoothie like Candy Corn (page 108). Most retail stores that have a kitchen section will sell a variety of cups. You can also find them easily online.

Liquids for Smoothies

COW'S MILK

My kids don't have any dairy intolerance or allergies, so cow's milk is the milk I use most often. Kids need fat, so I never use skim milk. I use 2% for my kids, but you can use whole milk if you are making the smoothie for a child two years old or younger. Cow's milk is a complete protein, containing the right proportions of all nine essential amino acids your body needs to form proteins. Cow's milk is high in protein, calcium, and vitamin B_{12}.

SOY MILK

Soy milk is not technically a milk; it's made from soybeans. Soy milk tends to be used by people with lactose intolerance, but it contains less protein than cow's milk. It is also lower in sugar and calories than cow's milk. Look for soy milk that is fortified with calcium and vitamins because they are not normally found in soy milk. There is some controversy surrounding soy milk, though; some studies indicate that it interferes with vitamin absorption.

RICE MILK

Rice milk is made by processing cooked rice. Rice milk contains no lactose, so it is an option for those with lactose intolerance, but it is high in carbohydrates and has little protein. It is naturally sweeter than other milks, but beware of added sugars. Rice milk is not normally a good source of vitamins, so look for rice milk fortified with vitamins and minerals.

COCONUT MILK BEVERAGE

I use the coconut milk beverage that's sold in shelf-stable boxes—*not* full-fat, canned coconut milk. The coconut milk beverage is thinner and easier to incorporate into a smoothie than the canned coconut milk. Coconut milk is lower in protein and calcium than cow's milk, but it is also lower in calories. It does have a light coconut flavor that will be recognizable in some smoothies, so keep that in mind if you are substituting it for cow's milk. Read the label to make sure that the product contains only coconut milk and filtered water. Do not substitute coconut water for coconut milk beverage in the smoothie recipes. For more information on coconut water—the juice from inside a coconut—please see the box on page 117.

ALMOND MILK

Almond milk is a popular alternative to regular milk because it is mild in flavor and has a consistency similar to cow's milk. It is lower in protein than cow's milk, and it is usually fortified so that the calcium content is similar to that of cow's milk. Almond milk is more nutrient-rich than some other milk alternatives, and as long as you don't have a nut allergy, it is a good substitute. Make sure you buy plain, unsweetened almond milk to use in these recipes; there can be a lot of added sugars in the flavored varieties.

What Milk Do You Want to Use?

In most cases, you can substitute one milk for another, depending on your kids' preferences and dietary needs. Just keep in mind that cow's milk, soy milk, rice milk, coconut milk, and almond milk have different flavor profiles and consistencies.

FRUIT JUICE

When buying juice for a smoothie, remember to always read the label to make sure the product is 100 percent juice, with no sugar or extras added. Juices like orange or apple juice are often found in the refrigerated section, but most grocery stores will have a designated section near the produce section for fresh and natural fruit juices, where you can find juices like pomegranate or acai juice.

When a recipe calls for lemon or lime juice, make sure you are squeezing fresh juice from the fruit yourself. The bottled versions often contain all kinds of preservatives and don't taste nearly as good as fresh juice.

VEGETABLE JUICE

The only vegetable juice that I typically use is carrot juice. I find that it's much easier to add to a smoothie than actual carrots. You can usually find it in the fresh fruit juice section of your grocery store.

WATER

Because I want my kids to get extra nutrients, I add milk or juice to the smoothies I make, but there is nothing wrong with using plain water. Sometimes you need a little liquid to get things moving, and water will work just fine. I'll also add water to cut the strong flavor of some ingredients such as grapefruit juice.

Fruits and Veggies for Smoothies

I use fruits and vegetables as the major bulk of my smoothies. That way I get the most bang for my buck when it comes to nutrition, and that's my main purpose in serving smoothies to my kids.

You'll notice that I use a lot of frozen fruit in my smoothies. It gives the smoothie that icy, thick texture we love. Whenever possible, I freeze the fruit myself. First, because I think it tastes better. I can wait until the fruit is at its peak ripeness before freezing it, ensuring that it is super sweet and perfect for smoothies. When you use fruit that is ripe and sweet, you won't need to add sweeteners. Stock up when fruit is in season and on sale. Fresh fruit will be cheaper than commercially frozen fruit, which I've found to be inconsistent. Sometimes it's nice and sweet; other times it will have little flavor.

There are a few fruits that I add fresh instead of frozen, such as apples and oranges. And when I add vegetables, they're always fresh.

Vegetables are actually quite easy to incorporate into smoothies since some of them have some natural sweetness while others have flavors mild enough to "hide" with other more prominent flavors. I love the sweetness beets and carrots bring. Vegetables such as spinach, broccoli, cauliflower, cabbage, and celery have flavors that easily blend when they are paired with bolder flavors. Cucumbers bring a refreshing flavor that is unique.

BERRIES

Wash them and then dry them in a single layer on a baking sheet lined with paper towels. Hull strawberries before washing and drying them. Once the berries are dried, transfer them to a baking sheet lined with parchment paper and put them in the freezer.

CHERRIES

Wash, dry, and pit cherries before freezing them.

GRAPES

Start with seedless grapes. Wash them and then dry them in a single layer on a baking sheet lined with paper towels. Then transfer them to a parchment-lined baking sheet and freeze them.

MELONS

I buy small or seedless watermelons so I don't have to pick out all the black seeds. Cut honeydew melons and cantaloupes in half and scoop out the

Freezing Fruit

Line a baking sheet with parchment paper. This ensures that the fruit doesn't freeze to the baking sheet.

Arrange the fruit in a single layer and transfer it to the freezer until it is frozen solid. Once the fruit is frozen, transfer it to a labeled freezer-safe zip-top plastic bag. Remove as much air as possible, and return the fruit to the freezer.

seeds. Cut the melons in wedges and then remove the rinds. Then cut the fruit into chunks before transferring it to a baking sheet lined with parchment paper and freezing the melon.

BANANAS

Bananas are one of the fruits I use the most in my smoothies. I love the consistency that frozen bananas give to smoothies, and so do my kids. I use two kinds.

Underripe bananas provide texture and a little sweetness without a lot of banana flavor. Look for bananas that are mostly green, with just a little yellow on the peel.

Ripe bananas provide that same texture, but with lots of banana flavor and lots of sweetness. I like mine really ripe, when there is more brown and black than there is yellow on the peel.

Peel the bananas and freeze them whole. Make sure to label the freezer bags so you will know which are ripe and which are underripe. They should be soft enough to slice when you take them out of the freezer; if not, let them sit on the counter for 5 minutes.

Apples

When I'm making a green smoothie, I tend to use a Granny Smith apple. Otherwise I just use whatever variety of apple I have on hand and that my kids like. I keep the peels on, but peel them if the added texture doesn't go over well with your kids.

MANGOES

Peel the fruit. Standing the fruit up vertically on your cutting board, carefully slice through one side of the mango, being careful not to cut into the pit. Make another cut on the other side of the pit. Trim off any flesh that remains on either side of the pit. Cut the mango flesh into chunks.

PAPAYAS

Peel, halve, and seed the papayas. Cut them into chunks.

PEACHES

Freestone peaches are the easiest to prep. Wash and dry the fruit, then cut it in half and remove the pit. Cut the peaches into slices. I don't think it's worth the hassle to peel peaches.

PEARS

Peel pears or not (I don't). Cut the fruit into vertical quarters and remove the core. Cut the pears into chunks.

PINEAPPLE

Cut off the top and bottom, then cut off the skin. Cut the pineapple into vertical quarters, then lay the quarters on their sides and cut off the core. Cut the pineapple quarters into chunks.

Additions

There are many things you can add to your smoothie to give it extra nutrition and flavor.

FLAXSEED

Flaxseed is high in essential omega-3 fatty acids, antioxidants, and fiber. I love adding flaxseed because it's easy to throw some into a smoothie, and it doesn't affect the taste or texture.

CHIA SEEDS

Chia seeds add a dose of essential omega-3 fatty acids, protein, and calcium. When adding chia seeds, make sure you consume the smoothie right away, as the seeds can absorb any water in the smoothie, giving it a gelatinous consistency. This will help to thicken up the smoothie, but it may create a texture that is not popular among kids.

YOGURT

Yogurt is one of my favorite additions. It gives a smoothie an element of creaminess and is a great source of protein, calcium, and live bacterial cultures, which are good for digestion. I always use plain Greek yogurt. Greek yogurt typically has two times more protein than regular yogurt. Plus its thick texture works really well in smoothies. If you'd prefer to use regular yogurt, go ahead, but remember that the smoothie will be thinner.

OATMEAL

Oatmeal is a great addition if you are looking for something to bulk up your smoothies and give them more staying power. Oatmeal is great for stabilizing blood sugar, which means your kids will stay fuller longer without having any blood sugar crashes.

NUT BUTTERS

Not only do different nut butters add great flavor to smoothies, they are also high in heart-healthy fats and protein. We have always loved peanut butter but recently we have fallen in love with almond butter. You can also look for cashew butter, or you can even find nut-free substitutes.

EXTRACTS

Extracts are a great way to add a lot of flavor without adding bulk or calories. My favorite is vanilla extract, as it is the easiest to combine with other flavors, but my kids also love mint, lemon, and coconut extracts. Make sure you are using a pure extract when possible, and remember that a small amount goes a long way toward flavoring a smoothie.

Sweeteners

I rely on ripe fruit and berries to sweeten most of my smoothies, but sometimes I need to add a bit of sweetener. I stick to my favorites—agave syrup, honey, dates, and pure maple syrup—but this is a great place to experiment to see what your kids like and what works well with your diets. Giving your kids foods containing natural sweeteners is better for them because their blood glucose levels will rise slowly and steadily. You will be avoiding the crash and subsequent hunger kids experience after eating store-bought snacks such as cookies, candies, and soda pop.

AGAVE SYRUP

This sweetener has the mildest flavor and therefore doesn't change the taste of the smoothie. Most agave syrups come from the blue agave plant, grown primarily in Mexico. It is one and a half times sweeter than sugar, so use it sparingly.

HONEY

Honey is also sweeter than sugar, so you don't have to use as much of it.

Different kinds of honey have different tastes, some of them very distinct and assertive. I use clover honey. When purchasing honey, read the label to make sure you are getting pure, natural honey without any additives.

PURE MAPLE SYRUP

Pure maple syrup makes a great sweetener, but it also has a distinct taste. I use it when I want that maple flavor. Maple syrup contains a good amount of healthy vitamins and minerals, so it is a good choice if you need to add a sweetener.

DRIED DATES

Dates are another one of my favorite sweeteners. It's easy to add one or two to your smoothie and blend away. If you have a cheaper blender, dates won't always blend completely, but macerating them a bit beforehand will help. I buy dates in the bulk section at my grocery store. They're fairly inexpensive and they will keep for several months in the pantry.

Breakfast Smoothies

Breakfast is always the toughest meal of the day for me. While I love breakfast foods, it just takes me too long to get moving in the morning to make a big breakfast for my family each day. Smoothies have become my favorite way to give my kids a healthy breakfast full of nutrition for a great start to the day. These smoothies work well as stand-alone breakfasts, or, if your kids need something more, these smoothies are good alongside a heartier dish.

Strawberry Banana Oatmeal

When I was a child, strawberries and bananas were my favorite flavor combination. My kids share that love—especially Abbi, who will never turn down anything with strawberries. She doesn't always love smoothies with lots of texture, but these flavors won her over.

MAKES 4 (8-OUNCE) SERVINGS

1 cup milk

2 cups frozen strawberries

1 frozen ripe banana

½ cup old-fashioned oats

1 tablespoon agave syrup or honey

1   Pour the milk into a blender. Add the strawberries. Cut the banana into slices and add it to the blender.

2   Add the oats and the sweetener, then blend until smooth.

Secret Spinach Strawberry Banana

The taste of spinach is so mild, and it pairs well with strawberry and banana. That makes spinach a great choice when you want to slip a serving of veggies into your kids' breakfast. This isn't the prettiest smoothie, so serve it in an opaque cup.

MAKES 4 (7-OUNCE) SERVINGS

1 cup milk

1 cup frozen strawberries

1 frozen ripe banana

2 cups loosely packed spinach leaves

1   Pour the milk into a blender. Add the frozen strawberries. Slice the banana and add it to the blender.

2   Top with the spinach and blend until smooth.

Strawberry Oats Coconut Chia

Oats are a great addition to a morning smoothie, as they keep the kids full for longer. Some people swear by grinding the oats beforehand so that they will blend in better, but I don't usually have the time to take that extra step, and for the most part my kids don't mind the extra texture. But if texture is an issue with your kids, run the oats in your blender until they are powdery before adding the other ingredients.

MAKES 4 (8-OUNCE) SERVINGS

2 cups coconut milk beverage (see page 14)

2 cups frozen strawberries

1 cup old-fashioned oats

¼ cup chia seeds

1 tablespoon agave syrup or honey

1   Pour the coconut milk into a blender. Add the strawberries, oats, chia seeds, and sweetener.

2   Blend until smooth. Serve immediately.

Strawberry Grapefruit

It took me a while to get my kids to eat grapefruit sections, but I found that slipping some grapefruit juice into a smoothie was a great way to get their palates familiar with the flavor. Now they love it. Here's a little trick: Start off with ½ cup grapefruit juice and 1½ cups water and work your way up to the full cup of juice.

MAKES 4 (9-OUNCE) SERVINGS

> 1 cup grapefruit juice
>
> 1 cup water
>
> 2 cups frozen strawberries
>
> 1 apple
>
> 2 tablespoons agave syrup or honey

1 Pour the grapefruit juice and water in a blender. Add the frozen strawberries. Core the apple, cut it into chunks, and add it to the blender.

2 Add the sweetener. Blend until smooth.

Berry Beet

This smoothie is one of my very favorites. With only three ingredients, it's super simple and full of flavor. The coconut milk adds creaminess and just a touch of coconut flavor, but it's the strawberries that really shine. The beet adds a bit of sweetness, as well as a beautiful pink color. Working with beets can be a little messy, and your hands may be stained all day, but this smoothie is totally worth it! Of course, you could wear latex or rubber gloves while you prep the beet.

MAKES 4 (9-OUNCE) SERVINGS

> 2 ¼ cups coconut milk beverage (see page 14)
> 3 cups frozen strawberries
> 1 medium raw beet

1   Pour the coconut milk into a blender. Add the strawberries.

2   Peel the beet, cut it into thin slices, and add it to the blender. Blend until smooth.

Blueberry Pomegranate

My kids love the fruity and tangy combination of blueberries and pomegranates. The antioxidants, minerals, and other nutrients in blueberries and pomegranates make this smoothie a power breakfast.

MAKES 4 (10-OUNCE) SERVINGS

2 cups pomegranate juice

3 cups frozen blueberries

1 cup ice cubes

1 Pour the pomegranate juice into a blender.

2 Add the blueberries and the ice and blend until smooth.

Berry, Beet, & Acai

This smoothie is packed with antioxidants, as well as a good boost of amino acids and omega-3 fatty acids from the acai juice. It's sweet and it's tart, and it will satisfy the kids' appetites. Look for acai juice in the fresh juice section of your grocery store.

MAKES 4 (8-OUNCE) SERVINGS

1½ cups acai juice

1 cup coconut water

1 cup frozen blueberries

1 small raw beet

1   Pour the acai juice and coconut water into the blender. Add the blueberries.

2   Peel the beet, cut it into thin slices, and add it to the blender. Blend until smooth.

About Acai Juice

The acai berry comes from the rain forests of Central and South America, where Brazilian natives have been using this fruit for hundreds of years for healing and to boost energy. It has been called a superfood because it contains antioxidants, amino acids, and omega fatty acids. It also packs a good amount of protein.

Acai tastes like a raspberry or blackberry with chocolate undertones. Not everyone loves the taste of the juice straight from the bottle, but it mixes well with other fruits and vegetables in smoothies. It looks like cloudy prune juice, but don't let the color deter you. When mixed with other ingredients in a smoothie, it adds a nice purple hue.

Check the label of acai juice products and make sure that the first ingredient is acai. Some brands are fortified with additional vitamins and minerals—which is great.

Beets in Smoothies

When I first started adding beets to smoothies, I roasted them. But I soon found out that it's a lot easier to just peel and thinly slice raw beets. Raw beets are a lot milder in flavor than cooked beets. While you wouldn't want to serve your kids a pure beet smoothie, beets pair well with berries and even chocolate. They add a mild sweetness and earthiness.

Beets are high in folate and give you a good dose of vitamins and antioxidants. I always use red beets because they add such a vibrant color, but you could use golden or candy cane beets if you like.

Very Berry

This one is for any kid who is a berry lover. I use a mixture of strawberries, cherries, raspberries, and blueberries, but you can substitute any mix of berries. The pomegranate juice adds a little bit of tartness and lots of sweetness.

MAKES 4 (9-OUNCE) SERVINGS

1½ cups pomegranate juice

¾ cup water

1½ cups frozen strawberries

¾ cup frozen cherries

¾ cup frozen raspberries

¾ cup frozen blueberries

1   Pour the pomegranate juice and water into a blender.

2   Add the strawberries, cherries, raspberries, and blueberries and blend until smooth.

Berry Blue

This filling smoothie is packed with antioxidants. Blackberries and blueberries are readily available, but if you are lucky enough to get your hands on other purple or blue berries like huckleberries, boysenberries, or marionberries, feel free to throw some of those in as well.

MAKES 4 (9-OUNCE) SERVINGS

2 ¼ cups milk

1 ½ frozen underripe bananas

¾ cup frozen blackberries

¾ cup frozen blueberries

⅓ cup old-fashioned oats

1   Pour the milk into a blender. Slice the bananas and add them to the milk.

2   Add the blackberries, blueberries, and oats. Blend until smooth.

Pomegranate Cherry

Pomegranate juice is one of my favorite liquids to add to smoothies, and my kids love it. It pairs perfectly with cherries, and the Greek yogurt gives the smoothie an irresistibly smooth and creamy texture.

MAKES 4 (10-OUNCE) SERVINGS

1½ cups pomegranate juice

2 cups frozen cherries

½ cup plain Greek yogurt

1 tablespoon honey

1 cup ice cubes

1   Pour the pomegranate juice into a blender.

2   Add the cherries, yogurt, and honey, followed by the ice. Blend until smooth.

Acai, Pomegranate, & Raspberry

Acai juice, pomegranate juice, and raspberries are full of antioxidants. I like to think of this as a sweet and tart superfood smoothie! And it is ready in a jiffy.

MAKES 4 (8-OUNCE) SERVINGS

1 cup acai juice
1 cup pomegranate juice
3 cups frozen raspberries

1 Pour the acai juice and pomegranate juice into a blender.

2 Add the raspberries and blend until smooth.

Cherry Banana

The combination of cherries and bananas with the creamy Greek yogurt make this a delicious, kid-friendly breakfast. My kids drink down these big, sweet servings in a flash.

MAKES 4 (10-OUNCE) SERVINGS

2 cups milk

2 cups frozen cherries

2 frozen ripe bananas

½ cup plain Greek yogurt

1   Pour the milk into a blender. Add the cherries.

2   Slice the bananas and add them to the blender along with the yogurt. Blend until smooth.

Peach Mango

I can't get enough of mangoes, and they pair so well with peaches that I just had to throw them together in a smoothie. There is a hint of the tropics in this smoothie, and my kids slurped it right down.

MAKES 4 (8-OUNCE) SERVINGS

2 cups milk

1 cup frozen sliced peaches

1 cup frozen mango chunks

1 frozen underripe banana

1 teaspoon vanilla extract

1   Pour the milk into a blender. Add the peaches and mangoes.

2   Slice the banana and add it to the blender along with the vanilla extract. Blend until smooth.

Papaya Ginger

Whenever I see a papaya at the market, I have to scoop it up so I will have it on hand for smoothies. Papayas have been known to give you an energy boost. The ginger adds a spicy bite to this smoothie.

MAKES 4 (8-OUNCE) SERVINGS

½ cup water

3 cups frozen papaya chunks

1 frozen underripe banana

1 teaspoon grated fresh ginger

1   Pour the water into a blender. Add the papayas.

2   Slice the banana and add it to the blender along with the ginger. Blend until smooth.

Under a Coconut Tree

Three ingredients—mangoes, papayas, and coconut milk—combine to create a smoothie that takes you straight to the tropics. For even more tropical flair, add a drop or two of coconut extract.

MAKES 4 (8-OUNCE) SERVINGS

> 2 cups coconut milk beverage (see page 14)
> 2 cups frozen papaya chunks
> 2 cups frozen mango chunks

1   Pour the milk into a blender.

2   Add the papayas and mangoes and blend until smooth.

Honeydew Cantaloupe

Melon smoothies have a luscious creaminess and are refreshing first thing in the morning. If your honeydew and cantaloupe are especially sweet, you may not even need the added sweetener.

MAKES 4 (9-OUNCE) SERVINGS

2¼ cups water or coconut water

1½ cups frozen cantaloupe chunks

1½ cups frozen honeydew chunks

1½ tablespoons agave syrup or honey, or to taste

1 Pour the water into a blender.

2 Add the cantaloupe, honeydew, and sweetener. Blend until smooth.

Melon Berry

My kids look forward to summer produce every year. There is nothing like picking up a ripe melon and eating it. Combining three of our favorite melons with strawberries creates one delicious breakfast. It's not particularly filling, so the servings are large.

MAKES 4 (10-OUNCE) SERVINGS

2½ cups coconut water

1 cup frozen seedless watermelon chunks

1 cup frozen cantaloupe chunks

1 cup frozen honeydew chunks

1 cup frozen strawberries

1 Pour the coconut water into a blender.

2 Add the watermelon, cantaloupe, honeydew, and strawberries and blend until smooth.

Soothing Citrus

If your kids like drinking orange juice with their breakfast, try substituting a glass of Soothing Citrus for that glass of OJ. Your children will start the day off with an extra dose of vitamin C, and the Greek yogurt tames that citrus tang!

MAKES 4 (8-OUNCE) SERVINGS

¾ cup orange juice

¼ cup grapefruit juice

2 tablespoons fresh lemon juice

2 tablespoons fresh lime juice

½ cup plain Greek yogurt

1 tablespoon agave syrup or honey

2 cups ice cubes

1   Combine the orange juice, grapefruit juice, lemon juice, and lime juice in a blender.

2   Add the yogurt and sweetener. Top with the ice and then blend until smooth.

Clementine Honey Lime

My kids eat clementines by the boxful. This sweet fruit is perfect in a smoothie because it is so juicy that you don't need to add any other liquid. Feel free to substitute mandarin oranges or tangerines or even navel oranges—but watch for seeds.

MAKES 4 (8-OUNCE) SERVINGS

7 or 8 clementines

2 tablespoons fresh lime juice

2 tablespoons honey

2 cups ice cubes

1   Peel the clementines and put them in a blender. Add the lime juice and honey.

2   Top with the ice and blend until smooth.

Cranberry Orange

Don't save the cranberry love for just the Thanksgiving table! Serve this festive smoothie on Thanksgiving morning to give the kids a healthy start before a day full of eating. Pure cranberry juice is pretty tart, but the orange juice is sweet enough to tame that tartness.

MAKES 4 (8-OUNCE) SERVINGS

1½ cups orange juice

1 cup 100% cranberry juice

2 cups ice cubes

1   Combine the orange juice and cranberry juice in a blender.

2   Top with the ice and blend until smooth.

Coconut Orange

This is a great tropical breakfast treat. I up the coconut flavor by adding a splash of coconut extract and give the smoothie a little zing with fresh ginger. The coconut flakes add a bit of texture.

MAKES 4 (9-OUNCE) SERVINGS

1 cup coconut milk beverage (see page 14)

2 cups orange juice

1 tablespoon agave syrup or honey

¼ teaspoon grated fresh ginger

¼ teaspoon coconut extract

2 cups ice cubes

2 tablespoons unsweetened coconut flakes, optional

1   Combine the coconut milk and orange juice in a blender. Add the sweetener, ginger, and coconut extract.

2   Top with the ice and blend until smooth. Stir in the coconut flakes, if you like.

Coconana

This dairy-free smoothie tastes more like dessert than breakfast! Bananas are a great carbohydrate that fill up little bellies and help keep them feeling full for longer.

MAKES 4 (8-OUNCE) SERVINGS

2 cups coconut milk beverage (see page 14)

2 or 3 pitted dates

2 frozen ripe bananas

1   Pour the coconut milk into a blender. Add the dates and let them soak in the coconut milk for about 10 minutes.

2   Cut the bananas into slices and add them to the blender. Blend until smooth.

Carrot Banana Berry

Carrot juice is slightly sweet and pairs well with many fruits. Adding it to smoothies is a great way to introduce a vegetable at breakfast. It is also easy to find at most major grocery stores. This combination of carrots, bananas, and blueberries is one that your kids will love.

MAKES 4 (9-OUNCE) SERVINGS

1 cup plain unsweetened almond milk

1 cup carrot juice

2 frozen ripe bananas

2 cups frozen blueberries

1 Pour the almond milk and carrot juice into a blender.

2 Slice the bananas and add them to the blender along with the blueberries. Blend until smooth.

Carrot Apple Ginger

I love carrots and apples together, and the ginger gives this smoothie an extra welcome oomph. This smoothie might be a tasty remedy for little tummy aches, since ginger has been shown to soothe an upset stomach.

MAKES 4 (9-OUNCE) SERVINGS

1 cup carrot juice

1 cup apple juice

1 large apple

1 teaspoon grated fresh ginger

2 cups ice cubes

1   Pour the carrot juice and apple juice into a blender. Core the apple, cut it into chunks, and add it to the blender.

2   Add the ginger, top with the ice, and blend until smooth.

Carrot Mango Orange

What says "good morning" better than orange juice? Combining it with carrot juice and mangoes! This very orange smoothie is filled with vitamins—perfect fuel for launching your morning.

MAKES 4 (10-OUNCE) SERVINGS

1½ cups orange juice

¾ cup carrot juice

3 cups frozen mango chunks

1   Pour the orange juice and carrot juice into a blender.

2   Add the mangoes and blend until smooth.

Carrot-Beet-Apple Treat

The flavors of carrots and apples stand out in this smoothie, with the pears and beets adding some sweetness. I've fallen in love with the earthy sweetness that raw beets add to smoothies. The vibrant color of this smoothie will be appealing to your kids.

MAKES 4 (9-OUNCE) SERVINGS

1 cup carrot juice
1 cup apple juice
2 cups frozen pear chunks
1 small raw beet
1 small apple

1 Pour the carrot juice and apple juice into a blender. Add the pears.

2 Peel the beet, cut it into thin slices, and add it to the blender.

3 Core the apple, cut it into chunks, and add it to the blender. Blend until smooth.

Lunchtime Smoothies

We often get stuck in the lunchtime sandwich rut. Whenever the kids start begging for something different, I know a smoothie will be a popular lunch choice! A smoothie will give your children a great midday boost, and if you can sneak in some extra vegetables, that's even better. I also love that smoothies can be portable for those days when the appointments and errands don't seem to end. Just stick the smoothies in a cup with a lid and a straw and the kids can drink their lunches on the go.

PB&J 68

Tropical Nut 69

Strawberry Peanut Butter 70

Honeydew Almond 72

Peach Almond 73

Kiwi Strawberry 75

Pear Berry 76

Spiced Pear 77

Creamy Pineapple 78

Green Pineapple Strawberry 79

Pineapple, Red Cabbage, & Banana 80

Banana Cauliflower 82

Beet Cucumber Apple 83

Beet Cherry Berry 84

Berry Broccoli 86

Greens & Berries 88

Avocado Vanilla 89

Avocado Pear 91

Double-Decker Tropical Avocado 92

Cucumber Lime 94

Cucumber Pineapple Kiwi 95

Spiced Carrot Orange 97

Sweet Potato, Mango, & Peach 98

PB&J

My kids ask for peanut butter and jelly sandwiches for lunch several times a week. If your kids love peanut butter and jelly as much as mine do, try serving this smoothie for lunch and watch smiles break out on their faces.

MAKES 4 (8-OUNCE) SERVINGS

2½ cups milk

3 frozen underripe bananas

3 tablespoons natural peanut butter

3 tablespoons 100% fruit spread

1   Pour the milk into a blender. Cut the bananas into slices and add them to the milk.

2   Add the peanut butter and fruit spread. Blend until smooth.

Tropical Nut

I don't know if I'd ever turn down a tropical smoothie, and I've passed this passion on to my kids. The almond milk and almond butter make this smoothie rich in vitamins, minerals, protein, and fiber—and it tastes great too.

MAKES 4 (8-OUNCE) SERVINGS

2 cups plain unsweetened almond milk

1 cup frozen pineapple chunks

1 cup frozen mango chunks

2 kiwis

2 tablespoons almond butter

1 Pour the almond milk into a blender. Add the pineapple and mangoes.

2 Peel and chop the kiwis and add them to the blender. Top with the almond butter. Blend until smooth.

Strawberry Peanut Butter

My daughter came up with the idea for this smoothie one day while she was eating a peanut butter and strawberry jelly sandwich for lunch. She asked if I would make her a strawberry smoothie and add some peanut butter. Who am I to turn down a five-year-old? She loved it, and it has become one of her favorites.

MAKES 4 (8-OUNCE) SERVINGS

1½ cups milk

2 cups frozen strawberries

3 tablespoons natural peanut butter

1   Pour the milk into a blender.

2   Add the strawberries and peanut butter and blend until smooth.

Honeydew Almond

I am convinced that just about every fruit pairs well with almonds. Make sure your frozen honeydew is nice and sweet so you won't need any added sweeteners. Sweet and nutty, this smoothie is one of our favorites!

MAKES 4 (9-OUNCE) SERVINGS

2 ¼ cups plain unsweetened almond milk

3 cups frozen honeydew melon chunks

3 tablespoons almond butter

1   Pour the almond milk into a blender.

2   Add the honeydew and almond butter. Blend until smooth.

Peach Almond

Fresh peaches are probably my favorite fruit, and my kids share that love. I buy peaches by the boxful when they are in season. The almond milk and almond butter accentuate the wonderful peachiness of this summertime smoothie.

MAKES 4 (8-OUNCE) SERVINGS

2 cups plain unsweetened almond milk

2 cups frozen sliced peaches

2 tablespoons almond butter

1 tablespoon agave syrup or honey

1   Pour the almond milk into a blender.

2   Add the peaches, followed by the almond butter and the sweetener. Blend until smooth.

Lunchtime Smoothies

73

Kiwi Strawberry

I'm pretty sure that kiwis and strawberries were meant to go together. Add some yogurt and you have a smoothie that's creamy, sweet, and refreshing. And I love the speckling of kiwi seeds throughout the smoothie.

MAKES 4 (8-OUNCE) SERVINGS

1½ cups milk

2 cups frozen strawberries

2 kiwis

½ cup plain Greek yogurt

1 tablespoon agave syrup or honey

1   Pour the milk into a blender. Add the strawberries.

2   Peel and slice the kiwis, then add them to the blender.

3   Add the yogurt and the sweetener and blend until smooth.

Pear Berry

This smoothie is filled with fiber and protein and will keep the kids satisfied for a long time. I have made this smoothie with both mixed berries and just blueberries and loved both versions, so feel free to use whatever berries you have on hand.

MAKES 4 (8-OUNCE) SERVINGS

1 cup milk

1 cup plain Greek yogurt

2 cups frozen pear chunks

2 cups frozen mixed berries

1   Pour the milk into a blender.

2   Add the yogurt, pears, and berries. Blend until smooth.

Spiced Pear

Pears were among the fruits that I thought I didn't like as a child. Obviously, I had never tried one of these Spiced Pear smoothies; otherwise I would have known how wrong I was! Luckily, my kids have loved pears since they were babies, so this smoothie is perfect for them. I throw in some flaxseed for added essential omega-3 fatty acids and fiber.

MAKES 4 (9-OUNCE) SERVINGS

2¼ cups plain unsweetened almond milk

1½ frozen underripe bananas

1½ cups frozen pear chunks

1½ tablespoons flaxseed

1½ teaspoons grated fresh ginger

¾ teaspoon ground cinnamon

1   Pour the almond milk into a blender. Slice the bananas and add them to the blender.

2   Add the pears, flaxseeds, ginger, and cinnamon. Blend until smooth.

Creamy Pineapple

Cottage cheese makes a smoothie thick and creamy, and it's a great way to work in some extra protein. Make sure you blend this smoothie thoroughly, so the cottage cheese will become completely smooth.

MAKES 4 (8-OUNCE) SERVINGS

1½ cups milk

1½ cups frozen pineapple chunks

¾ cup cottage cheese

2 teaspoons agave syrup or honey

1   Pour the milk into a blender.

2   Add the pineapple, cottage cheese, and sweetener. Blend until smooth.

Green Pineapple Strawberry

Something magical happens when you add tropical flavors to summertime strawberries. And the pineapple juice is strong enough to mask most of the bitter flavor of the kale in this smoothie. If you're looking for milder flavor, use spinach.

MAKES 4 (8-OUNCE) SERVINGS

2 cups pineapple juice

2 cups frozen strawberries

2 cups loosely packed chopped kale or spinach (stems removed)

1 Pour the pineapple juice into a blender.

2 Add the strawberries and then the greens. Blend until smooth.

Pineapple, Red Cabbage, & Banana

My daughter, who loves anything pink or purple, was smitten with the color of this smoothie. The red cabbage adds such a beautiful bright purple color. It also contributes a serving of vegetables to your meal, which is always a good thing! Red cabbage is mild and pairs well with the pineapple, so this smoothie is beautiful and very delicious as well.

MAKES 4 (8-OUNCE) SERVINGS

2 cups pineapple juice
2 cups shredded red cabbage
2 frozen ripe bananas

1   Pour the pineapple juice into a blender. Add the cabbage.

2   Slice the bananas, add them to the blender, and blend until smooth.

Banana Cauliflower

Cauliflower is a great source of fiber. It is a smart choice as an addition to smoothies because its flavor is mild. The kids won't even be able to taste it. The combination of banana and cinnamon is the standout flavor in this smoothie.

MAKES 4 (10-OUNCE) SERVINGS

1½ cups milk

2 frozen ripe bananas

1 cup cauliflower florets

¼ teaspoon ground cinnamon

1   Pour the milk into a blender. Slice the bananas and add them to the blender.

2   Top with the cauliflower and cinnamon and blend until smooth.

Beet Cucumber Apple

Cucumber makes this smoothie refreshing, while the beet gives the kids added energy to get through the rest of the day. The flavor of the pears isn't strong, but I include them because of their sweetness and the extra body they add to this smoothie.

MAKES 4 (10-OUNCE) SERVINGS

2 cups apple juice

1 cup peeled and diced seedless cucumber

1 medium raw beet

1 cup frozen pear chunks

2 cups ice cubes

1   Pour the apple juice into a blender. Add the cucumber.

2   Peel the beet, cut it into thin slices, and add it to the blender.

3   Add the pears, top with the ice, and blend until smooth.

Beet Cherry Berry

This smoothie might not be right for a "green" beginner, since the beets and kale make it quite earthy. My kids have grown to love this, though, and it's a great way to switch up your greens. For a milder smoothie, substitute spinach for the kale.

MAKES 4 (8-OUNCE) SERVINGS

1½ cups milk

1 small raw beet

¾ cup frozen cherries

¾ cup frozen strawberries

2 cups chopped kale (stems removed)

1   Pour the milk into a blender. Peel the beet, cut it into thin slices, and add it to the blender.

2   Add the cherries, strawberries, and kale. Blend until smooth.

Kale

While adults everywhere have seemed to jump on the kale band-wagon, it might be a little harder to get the kids to love kale. But now is a good time to get their palates acquainted with this nutrient-rich leafy green. It is often called one of the healthiest vegetables, filled with vitamin A, vitamin C, and vitamin K. It is also a great source of fiber.

Kale has a deep, earthy flavor, but it can sometimes be bitter, so it's not so easy to hide in a smoothie. When I started using kale, I would use only small amounts; as my kids grew accustomed to it, I added more and more. I tend to use whatever variety of kale is available at my grocery store, which is typically curly kale. It is best to wash the kale right before using it and dry it thoroughly. Then stem it and chop the leaves into smaller, more manageable pieces. Kale is harder to break down than spinach, so keep on blending your smoothie until it's completely smooth.

Berry Broccoli

Broccoli is one of the few vegetables my kids will eat, so I thought I'd try it out in a smoothie even though it's an unusual smoothie ingredient. It was a hit! Try this even if your kids say they don't like broccoli. You can barely taste it in this smoothie because the berries take center stage!

MAKES 4 (9-OUNCE) SERVINGS

2½ cups milk

3 cups mixed frozen berries

1 cup broccoli florets

1   Pour the milk into a blender.

2   Add the berries and broccoli and blend until smooth.

Greens & Berries

This "green" smoothie gets its greenness from both spinach and fresh broccoli. The orange juice and berries hide the taste of raw broccoli, so your kids won't even know it's there.

MAKES 4 (9-OUNCE) SERVINGS

3 cups orange juice

1½ cups mixed frozen berries

1 cup chopped broccoli florets

2 cups loosely packed spinach (stems removed)

1   Pour the orange juice into a blender. Add the berries and the broccoli.

2   Top with the spinach. Blend until smooth.

Avocado Vanilla

Avocados are full of healthy fats and protein and contain lots of fiber. They also make this smoothie creamy and smooth. It will help keep the kids going through the afternoon.

MAKES 4 (8-OUNCE) SERVINGS

2 cups milk

1 ripe avocado

1 tablespoon agave syrup, honey, or pure maple syrup

2 teaspoons vanilla extract

2 cups ice cubes

1. Pour the milk into a blender. Peel and seed the avocado, and add it to the blender along with the sweetener and vanilla extract.

2. Top with the ice and blend until smooth.

Prepping an Avocado

Start by washing and drying the fruit. Then, using a sharp knife, slice through the avocado lengthwise until you feel the pit. Carefully rotate the avocado, cutting around the pit. You should be able to pull the fruit apart into two halves, with the pit stuck in one half. Use a spoon to remove the pit. For smoothies, you don't need to slice or dice the avocado—just use a large spoon to scoop the flesh out of the skin and add it directly to the blender.

Avocado Pear

The first time I tried adding avocado to a smoothie, I wasn't sold. I used a whole avocado for two servings, and the flavor overpowered the other ingredients. I consulted my friends Carrian and Kristy—both of whom love avocados in smoothies—and realized that my proportions were off. After cutting down on the amount of avocado, I was convinced of the beauty of adding the fruit. Avocados provide a good amount of fiber, folate, and vitamin K, and they also promote nutrient absorption.

MAKES 4 (6-OUNCE) SERVINGS

2 cups milk

1 cup frozen pear chunks

Half a small, ripe avocado

1 teaspoon vanilla extract

1   Pour the milk into a blender and add the pears.

2   Peel and seed the avocado and add to it the blender.

3   Spoon in the vanilla and blend until smooth.

Double-Decker Tropical Avocado

This smoothie is great to serve in the depths of winter. There's a bottom layer of pineapple, mango, and kiwi made creamy by the addition of avocado, and the top layer is a froth of strawberries and coconut milk. Serve this in a clear cup.

MAKES 4 (9-OUNCE) SERVINGS

1½ cups pineapple juice

1½ cups frozen mango chunks

2 kiwis

Half a small, ripe avocado

¾ cup coconut milk beverage (see page 14)

1½ cups frozen strawberries

1 Pour the pineapple juice into a blender. Add the mangoes. Peel and dice the kiwis, peel and seed the avocado, and add them to the blender. Blend until smooth.

2 Divide the smoothie among four glasses. Rinse out the blender.

3 Combine the coconut milk and strawberries in the blender. Blend until smooth.

4 Add a spoonful or two of the coconut strawberry smoothie to the top of each glass, dividing the mixture evenly among the glasses, and serve.

Cucumber Lime

This delicious, refreshing smoothie is perfect in the summertime, because cucumber helps to keep you hydrated. The lime juice adds an edge of tartness that my kids love.

MAKES 4 (9-OUNCE) SERVINGS

1½ cups water

¾ cup peeled, diced seedless cucumber

2½ tablespoons fresh lime juice

4 or 5 mint leaves

3 cups ice cubes

1   Pour the water into a blender. Add the cucumber, lime juice, and mint.

2   Top with the ice and blend until smooth.

Cucumber Pineapple Kiwi

Cucumber adds freshness and some vitamin B to this smoothie. If you think your kids don't like cucumber, this is the place to introduce it. The pineapple juice has such a strong flavor that they may not even know the cucumber is there.

MAKES 4 (8-OUNCE) SERVINGS

2 cups pineapple juice

½ cup peeled, diced seedless cucumber

2 kiwis

2 cups ice cubes

1 Pour the pineapple juice into a blender. Add the cucumber.

2 Peel and slice the kiwis and add them to the blender. Top with the ice and blend until smooth.

Spiced Carrot Orange

I could drink this smoothie year-round, but the spices make this especially appealing during the cold months. The complementary flavors of carrots and oranges make this a family favorite.

MAKES 4 (8-OUNCE) SERVINGS

1 cup carrot juice

1 cup orange juice

¼ teaspoon ground cinnamon

Dash of grated nutmeg

Dash of ground cardamom

3 cups ice cubes

1   Pour the carrot juice and orange juice into a blender.

2   Add the cinnamon, nutmeg, and cardamom. Top with the ice and blend until smooth.

Sweet Potato, Mango, & Peach

My brother is allergic to white potatoes, but he can eat sweet potatoes, so growing up we often had sweet potatoes on the dinner table. I usually skipped them. Little did I know how much I was missing. Today they are one of my favorite foods, and I want my kids to grow up enjoying them instead of ignoring them. This smoothie is a great way to introduce sweet potatoes, since their flavor combines well with mangoes and peaches.

MAKES 4 (8-OUNCE) SERVINGS

> 2 cups coconut milk beverage (see page 14)
> 1 cup frozen mango chunks
> 1 cup frozen sliced peaches
> 1 cup mashed, cooked sweet potato

1   Pour the coconut milk into a blender.

2   Add the mangoes, peaches, and sweet potato. Blend until smooth.

Snacktime Smoothies

I know I'm not alone when it comes to having kids who are always on the lookout for snacks. If you want something more healthful than fruit snacks and peanut butter crackers for the kids, smoothies are a great choice. They are also filling enough to hold kids over until dinnertime without ruining their appetites. Try them out as an easy after-school snack or a midday pick-me-up.

Chocolate Peanut Butter

This is the perfect smoothie to offer your kids after they have spent the day playing outside. It's filling, and the peanut butter packs it with protein. It will give your kids the energy they need to get back out and play!

MAKES 4 (8-OUNCE) SERVINGS

2 cups milk

2 frozen underripe bananas

2 tablespoons unsweetened cocoa powder

2 tablespoons natural peanut butter

2 tablespoons honey

1   Pour the milk into a blender. Slice the bananas and add them to the milk.

2   Add the cocoa, peanut butter, and honey. Blend until smooth.

Cherry Chocolate

Every Christmas when I was growing up, I would get a box of chocolate-covered cherries from my parents. I think that is where my love of cherries and chocolate started, and it continues to this day. And now I'm passing along my love of this flavor combination to my children!

MAKES 4 (8-OUNCE) SERVINGS

1½ cups milk

2 pitted dates

1¼ cups frozen cherries

1 frozen underripe banana

1 tablespoon unsweetened cocoa powder

1 Pour the milk into a blender. Add the dates and let them soak for 10 minutes.

2 Cut the banana into slices, and add it to the blender. Add the cocoa powder. Blend until smooth.

Candy Corn

When October hits, it's all about candy corn in our house. With three layers—banana topped by mango-carrot topped by pineapple—this smoothie looks like candy corn, but it's much healthier. Serve it in clear cups so the kids can see the layers.

MAKES 4 (9-OUNCE) SERVINGS

½ cup milk

1 frozen underripe banana

¾ cup carrot juice

1 cup frozen mango chunks

¾ cup pineapple juice

1 cup frozen pineapple chunks

1   Place 4 clear cups in the freezer.

2   Pour the milk into a blender. Slice the banana and add it to the blender. Blend until smooth. Remove the cups from the freezer and spoon the banana mixture evenly into the bottom of each of the cups. Return the cups to the freezer for 5 to 10 minutes.

3   Rinse out the blender. Pour in the carrot juice. Add the mangoes and blend until smooth. Take the cups out of the freezer and spoon the orange layer evenly into the cups. Return to the freezer for 5 to 10 minutes.

4   Rinse out the blender. Pour in the pineapple juice, add the pineapple, and blend until smooth. Spoon evenly into the cups and serve.

Candy Cane

It wouldn't be the holidays without candy canes around every corner. While Abbi can do without them (she's not a fan of anything minty), Easton is a mint lover. The only thing that would make him love this smoothie more would be if he had a candy cane to stir it with!

MAKES 4 (7-OUNCE) SERVINGS

1½ cups coconut milk beverage (see page 14)

2 frozen underripe bananas

⅛ teaspoon peppermint extract

1 tablespoon agave syrup or pure maple syrup, optional

1   Pour the coconut milk into a blender. Slice the bananas and add them to the milk, followed by the peppermint extract. Blend until smooth.

2   Taste and add sweetener if desired.

Cashew Vanilla

Cashews make this smoothie particularly thick and creamy, so your kids will think they are drinking a vanilla milkshake. The trick is blending the smoothie twice. It's a great afternoon pick-me-up!

MAKES 4 (8-OUNCE) SERVINGS

2 cups coconut milk beverage (see page 14)

⅔ cup raw unsalted cashews

2 frozen underripe bananas

1 teaspoon vanilla extract

½ teaspoon ground cinnamon

1 Pour the coconut milk into a blender. Add the cashews and soak them in the coconut milk for at least 15 minutes. Blend until smooth.

2 Slice the bananas and add them to the milk, along with the vanilla and cinnamon. Blend until smooth.

The Smoothest Smoothies

If you're not using a top-of-the-line blender like a Blendtec, you may have difficulty making ingredients such as dates, oatmeal, and nuts completely smooth. Here's my tip.

First, soak dates, oatmeal, or nuts in the smoothie's liquid ingredient for 10 to 15 minutes. Then blend them until smooth before adding the rest of the ingredients and blending again.

Vanilla Honey Nut

For some reason, my kids are always asking for a bowl of cereal for an afternoon snack. I talk them out of it, telling them that cereal is for breakfast. So I was very happy when I developed this smoothie and realized that it tasted just like their favorite honey nut cereal. They don't ask for cereal in the afternoon anymore; they want this smoothie!

MAKES 4 (8-OUNCE) SERVINGS

2 cups almond milk

2 frozen underripe bananas

2 tablespoons almond butter

2 tablespoons honey

1 teaspoon vanilla extract

1   Pour the almond milk into a blender. Slice the bananas and add them to the blender.

2   Add the almond butter, honey, and vanilla extract. Blend until smooth.

Horchata

Horchata is a popular Mexican drink made with rice and almonds. I cheat a little with this smoothie version: I use rice milk and almond butter instead of going through the long process of grinding and soaking and straining rice and almonds. Your kids will love the flavor, and you will be happy about how easy it is to throw together!

MAKES 4 (8-OUNCE) SERVINGS

2 cups rice milk

2 frozen underripe bananas

2 teaspoons almond butter

2 teaspoons vanilla extract

¼ teaspoon ground cinnamon

1   Pour the rice milk into a blender. Slice the bananas and add them to the blender.

2   Add the almond butter, vanilla extract, and cinnamon. Blend until smooth.

Spiced Cider

In the cold weather months I like to make a big batch of spiced cider to have on hand when my family needs to warm up after being out in the cold. I've discovered that the kids love this icy-cold version of their favorite spiced cider in the hot summer months!

MAKES 4 (9-OUNCE) SERVINGS

3 cups apple cider
½ teaspoon pumpkin pie spice
2 cups ice cubes

1 Pour the apple cider into a blender. Add the pumpkin pie spice.

2 Top with the ice and blend until smooth.

Coconut Lime

Coconut and lime scream tropical. The coconut milk beverage brings so much more to this smoothie than a tropical flavor. It is a rich source of iron and potassium and is filled with important vitamins like niacin and folate. Sprinkle the tops of the smoothies with some shredded unsweetened coconut for a fun touch.

MAKES 4 (6-OUNCE) SERVINGS

1 cup coconut milk beverage (see page 14)

¼ cup fresh lime juice

2 tablespoons agave syrup or honey

¼ teaspoon coconut extract

1 cup ice cubes

Shredded unsweetened coconut, optional

1   Pour the coconut milk into a blender. Add the lime juice, sweetener, and coconut extract.

2   Pour in the ice and blend until smooth. Top each serving with shredded coconut, if you like.

Minted Lime

I like to keep fresh mint on hand just for smoothies like this one.
Mint dresses up the smoothie, making it feel a little special.
The lime and mint combined with coconut water make a light,
refreshing smoothie that the kids love on a warm afternoon.

MAKES 4 (9-OUNCE) SERVINGS

2 cups coconut water

3 tablespoons fresh lime juice

3 tablespoons agave syrup or honey

5 or 6 mint leaves

3 cups ice cubes

1   Pour the coconut water into a blender. Add the lime juice,
honey, and mint.

2   Top with the ice and blend until smooth.

About Coconut Water

Coconut water is the clear liquid that comes from the center of a
coconut. It has a light, nutty flavor.

Coconut water has been on the rise as a natural substitute for
sports drinks because of its high potassium and mineral content. It is
naturally fat- and cholesterol-free and has as much potassium as a
banana. Look for coconut water that is unsweetened and is labeled as
100 percent coconut water.

Green Apple Coconut Banana

I leave the peel on when I use apples in smoothies. Apple peels provide extra nutrition, and I like the texture they add. I use a green apple in this smoothie in keeping with the "green" of the smoothie, but substitute whatever kind of apple you have on hand.

MAKES 4 (6-OUNCE) SERVINGS

1 cup coconut milk beverage (see page 14)

1 frozen ripe banana

1 Granny Smith apple

1 cup spinach leaves

½ cup ice cubes

1 Pour the coconut milk into a blender. Slice the banana and add it to the blender.

2 Core the apple, cut it into chunks, and add it to the blender along with the spinach.

3 Top with the ice and blend until smooth.

Cucumber Apple Mint

I think you can guess that I like the combination of cucumbers and mint, but I've found that the kids like it only if the cucumbers are peeled and if I use a seedless variety. The apple juice and ice give this smoothie a slushy consistency, which is perfect on a hot afternoon.

MAKES 4 (8-OUNCE) SERVINGS

2 cups apple juice

½ cup peeled and diced seedless cucumber

3 or 4 mint leaves

2 cups ice cubes

1 Pour the apple juice into a blender. Add the cucumber and mint.

2 Top with the ice and blend until smooth.

Piña Colada

Take your kids on a tropical vacation without even leaving the kitchen with this Piña Colada smoothie. Frozen pineapple chunks thicken up the smoothie and add sweetness, and a few drops of coconut extract boost the coconut flavor. When you can't take them to the beach, this is a great substitute!

MAKES 4 (9-OUNCE) SERVINGS

2 ¼ cups coconut milk beverage (see page 14)
3 ½ cups frozen pineapple chunks
¾ teaspoon coconut extract

1 Pour the coconut milk into the blender.

2 Add the pineapple and coconut extract. Blend until smooth.

Chocolate Coconut

You see the combination of chocolate and coconut in cookies and candy all the time. Well, they pair perfectly in a smoothie too! You'll need a little added sweetness, and dates are a perfect way to sweeten anything made with chocolate.

MAKES 4 (8-OUNCE) SERVINGS

2 cups coconut milk beverage (see page 14)

4 pitted dates

2 frozen underripe bananas

¼ cup unsweetened cocoa powder

½ teaspoon coconut extract

1 Pour the coconut milk into a blender. Add the dates and soak them in the coconut milk for 10 minutes.

2 Slice the bananas and add them to the blender. Add the cocoa and coconut extract and blend until smooth.

Mango Lassi

A mango lassi is a popular drink from India and Pakistan. You usually find lassis on the menu at Indian and Pakistani restaurants, so I thought it would be fun to make them at home. The pinch of cinnamon and cardamom give this drink an extra wow factor.

MAKES 4 (6-OUNCE) SERVINGS

1¼ cups milk

½ cup plain Greek yogurt

2 cups frozen mango chunks

1 tablespoon honey

Pinch of ground cinnamon

Pinch of ground cardamom

1   Pour the milk into a blender.

2   Add the yogurt, mangoes, honey, cinnamon, and cardamom. Blend until smooth.

Creamy Lemon

I try to sneak lemon into just about everything because I love it so much. So while I originally created this smoothie for myself, I quickly discovered that my kids loved it just as much!

MAKES 4 (8-OUNCE) SERVINGS

1 cup milk

½ cup plain Greek yogurt

3 tablespoons fresh lemon juice

2 tablespoons agave syrup or honey

1¾ cups ice cubes

1 Pour the milk into a blender. Add the yogurt, lemon juice, and sweetener.

2 Top with the ice and blend until smooth.

Lemon Poppy Seed

Lemons and poppy seeds are a popular combination in baked goods, so I thought it would be fun to see how they would work in a smoothie. The result is a sweet-and-sour smoothie that my kids fell for right away. The lemon flavor is light, so if you want a more pronounced lemon flavor, add a little pure lemon extract.

MAKES 4 (10-OUNCE) SERVINGS

2 cups almond milk

½ cup fresh lemon juice

2 tablespoons pure maple syrup

2 teaspoons poppy seeds

1 teaspoon vanilla extract

4 cups ice cubes

½ teaspoon lemon extract, optional

1   Pour the almond milk into a blender. Add the lemon juice, maple syrup, poppy seeds, and vanilla extract.

2   Top with the ice and blend until smooth. If you want more lemon flavor, add the lemon extract.

Strawberry Lemonade

Most kids love strawberry lemonade all summer long, right? Here's my solution for turning a favorite summer drink into a refreshing snack that is free of added sugars and that will give your kids vitamins and minerals on a hot day.

MAKES 4 (9-OUNCE) SERVINGS

2 cups water

3 pitted dates

3 cups frozen strawberries

4 tablespoons fresh lemon juice

1   Pour the water into a blender. Add the dates and let them soak for 10 minutes.

2   Add the strawberries and lemon juice and blend until smooth.

Creamsicle

I remember the first time I encountered the creamy orange flavor of a Creamsicle when I was a kid. As an afternoon snack, this creamy and delicious smoothie is a lot better for your kids than an ice cream bar!

MAKES 4 (8-OUNCE) SERVINGS

1½ cups orange juice

½ cup milk

1 frozen underripe banana

1 teaspoon vanilla extract

2 cups ice cubes

1   Combine the orange juice and milk in a blender. Cut the banana into slices and add it to the blender along with the vanilla extract.

2   Top with the ice and blend until smooth.

Blackberry Cinnamon

This smoothie is best made with blackberries that are frozen when they are super ripe and juicy. The fragrant and warm flavor of cinnamon makes me think of blueberry cobbler.

MAKES 4 (8-OUNCE) SERVINGS

2 cups milk

1 cup plain Greek yogurt

2 cups frozen blackberries

1 tablespoon honey

1 teaspoon ground cinnamon

1 teaspoon vanilla extract

1   Pour the milk into a blender.

2   Add the yogurt and blackberries, then the honey, cinnamon, and vanilla extract. Blend until smooth.

Watermelon Coconut Water

This smoothie is a perfect treat for a summer afternoon. Most summertime watermelons are plenty sweet, but if yours isn't, add a little bit of agave syrup or honey to sweeten up this smoothie. You could also replace the coconut water with plain water for an experience of pure watermelon heaven.

MAKES 4 (9-OUNCE) SERVINGS

1¾ cups coconut water

3 cups frozen watermelon chunks

1 Pour the coconut water into a blender.

2 Add the watermelon chunks and blend until smooth.

Pineapple Celery

Celery in a smoothie? You bet! It may seem like a strange ingredient, but celery actually works quite well in this smoothie. It adds welcome fiber, but its flavor is elusive. Your kids will be wondering what the secret ingredient is.

MAKES 4 (10-OUNCE) SERVINGS

1 cup pineapple juice

2 celery ribs, thinly sliced

2 frozen underripe bananas

2 cups frozen pineapple chunks

1   Pour the pineapple juice into a blender and add the celery.

2   Slice the bananas and add them to the blender, along with the frozen pineapple. Blend until smooth.

Tutti-Frutti

This is by far Abbi's favorite smoothie. Maybe because of the strawberries, or maybe because of all of the sweet fruit. Regardless, when you drink this smoothie, any time of the year will feel like summertime!

MAKES 4 (9-OUNCE) SERVINGS

2 cups water or coconut water

1 cup frozen watermelon chunks

1 cup frozen strawberries

1 cup frozen pineapple chunks

1 cup frozen mango chunks

1   Pour the water into a blender.

2   Add the watermelon, strawberries, pineapple, and mangoes. Blend until smooth.

Tropical Green

This smoothie is a great way to fill little bellies with all kinds of healthy things at snacktime. My kids love fruit, and by including greens you feed your kids an extra vegetable they won't even know they're eating. You can use spinach or kale—whichever green your kids prefer.

MAKES 4 (8-OUNCE) SERVINGS

2 cups water

1 cup frozen mango chunks

1 cup frozen pineapple chunks

2 cups loosely packed spinach or chopped kale (stems removed)

2 tablespoons agave syrup or honey, optional

1   Pour the water into a blender. Add the mangoes, the pineapple, and the greens.

2   Blend until smooth. Taste and add sweetener, if you like.

Peachy Green

This smoothie is perfectly green and full of peach flavor. Even though it's green, your kids will never know that this smoothie is packed with healthy spinach because the flavor of spinach is so mild. The ginger adds a hint of spiciness that keeps the smoothie interesting.

MAKES 4 (9-OUNCE) SERVINGS

2 cups coconut milk beverage (see page 14)

2 cups frozen sliced peaches

2 frozen underripe bananas

1 teaspoon grated fresh ginger

2 cups loosely packed spinach leaves

1   Pour the coconut milk into a blender. Add the peaches.

2   Slice the bananas and add them to the blender. Add the ginger and then the spinach. Blend until smooth.

Dessert Smoothies

Let's face it: Dessert is usually the favorite part of the meal for both kids and adults. But serving dessert doesn't mean you have to give your kids something that is full of sugar and empty calories! The goal of these smoothies is to give your kids a sweet treat that is better for them than a cookie. Although I love to splurge and serve my family a really good dessert every once in a while, I try not to make it a daily habit. These smoothies are a great way to give the kids dessert that you can feel good about.

Oatmeal Raisin

Oatmeal raisin cookies are one of my very favorites. The flavors that I love really come through in this smoothie, especially the hint of cinnamon. This smoothie is thicker than most, because of the oats and the raisins; add a little more milk if you want a thinner smoothie.

MAKES 4 (6-OUNCE) SERVINGS

2 cups milk

1 cup old-fashioned oats

½ cup raisins

2 frozen underripe bananas

¼ teaspoon ground cinnamon

1 Pour the milk into a blender. Add the oats and the raisins and let them soak for 10 minutes.

2 Turn on the blender and process the oats and raisins until they have broken down and become mostly smooth.

3 Slice the bananas and add them to the blender along with the cinnamon. Blend until smooth.

Cookies & Cream

In my house, we are obsessed with everything cookies and cream, so it was a given that we would love a cookies and cream smoothie. My grocery store has a sugar-free section in the cookie aisle, and sugar-free chocolate chip cookies aren't hard to find. They add some sweetness, a little hint of chocolate, and great cookie flavor. If your kids want it to feel more like a milkshake, blend the cookies only until they are just broken up, leaving small chunks of cookies. This is a sure way to satisfy a sweet tooth!

MAKES 4 (8-OUNCE) SERVINGS

2 cups milk

4 frozen underripe bananas

4 ounces sugar-free chocolate chip cookies

2 teaspoons vanilla extract

1   Pour the milk into a blender. Slice the bananas and add them to the blender.

2   Add the cookies and vanilla extract and blend until smooth.

Thin Mint

Who doesn't love the famous mint and chocolate cookies? Instead of giving the kids cookies, you can give them this healthy smoothie at any time of the year! I use dates to sweeten this smoothie and sneak in some spinach—so the kids get a little vegetable even for dessert.

MAKES 4 (8-OUNCE) SERVINGS

1½ cups milk

4 or 5 pitted dates

2 tablespoons unsweetened cocoa powder

¼ teaspoon peppermint extract

1 cup loosely packed spinach leaves

2 cups ice

1   Pour the milk into a blender. Add the dates and let them soak for 10 minutes.

2   Add the cocoa powder, peppermint extract, and then the spinach. Top with the ice and blend until smooth.

Dessert Smoothies

147

Snickerdoodle

I just had to take one of the most popular cookies and turn it into a smoothie! We are a family of snickerdoodle lovers, and the sweetness and cinnamon flavor of the beloved cookie shines through in this creamy smoothie.

MAKES 4 (8-OUNCE) SERVINGS

2 cups milk

4 frozen underripe bananas

4 tablespoons pure maple syrup

3 tablespoons almond butter

2 teaspoons vanilla extract

2 teaspoons ground cinnamon

1 Pour the milk into a blender. Slice the bananas and add them to the blender.

2 Add the maple syrup, almond butter, vanilla extract, and cinnamon. Blend until smooth.

Peach Melba

Peach Melba is a classic dessert that combines sugared peaches, raspberry sauce, and vanilla ice cream. There is a reason this dessert is so popular: The combination of raspberries and peaches is out of this world. I like to keep the flavor of this smoothie light and bright, but if you want to mimic the ice cream in the original dessert, add some Greek yogurt.

MAKES 4 (9-OUNCE) SERVINGS

3 cups water

1 cup frozen raspberries

1 cup frozen sliced peaches

1   Pour the water into a blender.

2   Add the raspberries and peaches and blend until smooth.

Strawberry Shortcake

I look forward to fresh local strawberries every summer. I love being able to pick up tons of them from the farmer's market when they are fresh and cheap so that I can freeze them to enjoy in our smoothies all year long. They are best served on shortcake with lots of whipped cream. This smoothie is a nutritious way to enjoy that strawberry shortcake flavor any day of the year.

MAKES 4 (8-OUNCE) SERVINGS

2 cups milk

3 cups frozen strawberries

2 ounces sugar-free shortbread cookies

1 teaspoon vanilla extract

1 Pour the milk into a blender. Add the frozen strawberries.

2 Add the cookies and the vanilla extract and blend until smooth.

Raspberry Cheesecake

Cheesecake is one of my favorite things to make for the kids, but I don't make it often because it isn't the healthiest dessert. In this rich smoothie we get to enjoy all the flavors of a cheesecake without the guilt.

MAKES 4 (8-OUNCE) SERVINGS

2 cups milk

2 pitted dates

2 cups frozen raspberries

1 ounce cream cheese

1   Pour the milk into a blender. Add the dates and let them soak for 10 minutes.

2   Add the raspberries and cream cheese and blend until smooth.

Carrot Cake

When springtime comes and we start talking about our Easter dinner, my oldest begs for carrot cake. What could be a better alternative than this heavenly smoothie, filled with the best carrot cake flavors? It is perfectly acceptable to enjoy your carrot cake smoothie as a snack—or even for breakfast!

MAKES 4 (9-OUNCE) SERVINGS

- 1¼ cups carrot juice
- ¾ cup milk
- 1½ frozen underripe bananas
- ¾ teaspoon vanilla extract
- ½ teaspoon ground cinnamon
- ¾ cup ice cubes

1 Pour the carrot juice and milk into a blender. Slice the bananas and add them to the blender, followed by the vanilla extract and cinnamon.

2 Top with the ice and blend until smooth.

Dessert Smoothies

155

Red Velvet Cake

If you know me, you know I'm obsessed with all things red velvet. I won't use beets in red velvet cake, because I've tried and I've found that they interfere with the light chocolate and buttermilk flavor. But I make an exception in this smoothie. Not only does the beet give the smoothie a beautiful pink hue, it also makes this smoothie taste like red velvet cake in a glass!

MAKES 4 (8-OUNCE) SERVINGS

1½ cups milk

Half a medium raw beet

2 tablespoons cream cheese

3 teaspoons unsweetened cocoa powder

1½ tablespoons agave syrup or honey

1 teaspoon vanilla extract

2 cups ice cubes

1   Pour the milk into a blender. Peel the beet, cut it into thin slices, and add it to the blender.

2   Add the cream cheese, cocoa powder, sweetener, and vanilla. Top with the ice and blend until smooth.

Gingerbread

This creamy banana smoothie tastes just like a Christmas treat. The molasses underscores the gingerbread flavor. Make sure to use a mild or light molasses; blackstrap molasses has a robust flavor that might be too strong for kids.

MAKES 4 (6-OUNCE) SERVINGS

1 cup milk

1 frozen underripe banana

2 teaspoons molasses

2 teaspoons agave syrup, honey, or pure maple syrup

1 teaspoon vanilla extract

1 teaspoon pumpkin pie spice

2 cups ice cubes

1   Pour the milk into a blender. Slice the banana and add it to the blender.

2   Add the molasses, sweetener, vanilla extract, and pumpkin pie spice. Top with the ice and blend until smooth.

Caramel Apple

My kids ask for caramel apples when we visit the county or state fair. But they have so much sugar. Now I can offer them an alternative with a lot less sugar—this caramel-flavored, apple-sweet smoothie.

MAKES 4 (8-OUNCE) SERVINGS

¾ cup milk

¼ cup apple juice

1 apple

1 tablespoon sugar-free caramel syrup

2 cups ice cubes

1   Pour the milk and apple juice into a blender.

2   Core the apple, cut it into chunks, and add it to the blender. Drizzle with the caramel syrup, top with the ice, and blend until smooth.

Dessert Smoothies

Apple Pie

My mom is known for her apple pie. When I was a child it was always one of my holiday favorites. While nothing will rival mom's apple pie, my kids will tell you that this is one of their favorite fall smoothies!

MAKES 4 (8-OUNCE) SERVINGS

¼ cup apple cider

¼ cup plain Greek yogurt

2 medium apples

2 frozen underripe bananas

¼ teaspoon ground cinnamon

Dash of grated nutmeg

Dash of ground cardamom

1 cup ice cubes

1 Pour the apple cider into a blender and add the yogurt. Core the apples, cut them into chunks, and add them to the blender.

2 Slice the bananas and add them to the blender. Sprinkle the cinnamon, nutmeg, and cardamom over the bananas. Top with the ice and blend until smooth.

Banana Cream Pie

Creamy banana and shortbread cookies make this smoothie taste like an indulgent dessert. You might even be able to convince your kids that they are sipping a milkshake instead of a smoothie!

MAKES 4 (8-OUNCE) SERVINGS

2 cups milk

2 frozen ripe bananas

1 ounce sugar-free shortbread cookies

1 teaspoon vanilla extract

1   Pour the milk into a blender. Cut the bananas into slices and add them to the blender.

2   Add the cookies and vanilla extract. Blend until smooth.

Pumpkin Pie

If there is one pie that must be on my table at Thanksgiving, it is pumpkin pie. It's a tradition that I don't ever want to give up! Now my kids can savor those traditional Thanksgiving flavors in this smoothie at any time of the day, and at any time of the year.

MAKES 4 (9-OUNCE) SERVINGS

2 cups milk

1 cup pumpkin puree

2 frozen underripe bananas

2 tablespoons pure maple syrup

1 teaspoon vanilla extract

1 teaspoon pumpkin pie spice

1 cup ice cubes

1   Pour the milk into a blender. Add the pumpkin puree. Slice the bananas and add them to the blender.

2   Add the maple syrup, vanilla extract, and pumpkin pie spice. Top with the ice and blend until smooth.

Sweet Potato Pie

This smoothie tastes just like sweet potato pie—a favorite Southern holiday staple. Thick and spicy with just the right amount of sweetness, it is a guilt-free way to re-experience a favorite holiday pie!

MAKES 4 (8-OUNCE) SERVINGS

2 cups almond milk

2 frozen underripe bananas

⅔ cup mashed cooked sweet potato

¼ teaspoon pumpkin pie spice

1 tablespoon agave syrup, honey, or pure maple syrup, optional

1   Pour the almond milk into a blender. Slice the bananas and add them to the blender.

2   Add the sweet potato and pumpkin pie spice. Blend until smooth. Taste and add sweetener, if you like.

Key Lime Pie

Key limes aren't always as easy to find as their Persian cousins, but it's worth the effort to find them because they're less tart. This smoothie's coconut milk and banana mimic the creamy smoothness of a key lime pie's rich egg yolks and sweetened condensed milk. Your family will enjoy the flavor and benefit from the natural sweetness of this yummy dessert.

MAKES 4 (6-OUNCE) SERVINGS

1 cup coconut milk beverage (see page 14)

1 frozen underripe banana

2 tablespoons key lime juice (or fresh lime juice)

1 cup ice cubes

1 to 2 teaspoons agave syrup or honey

1 Pour the coconut milk into a blender. Slice the banana and add it to the blender, along with the key lime juice.

2 Top with the ice and blend until smooth. Add sweetener to taste.

Maple Cream

If your kids are fans of milkshakes, they will love this smoothie. Even I'm happy to have one of these for dessert! You would never guess that this smoothie is much better for you than an actual milkshake.

MAKES 4 (8-OUNCE) SERVINGS

2 cups almond milk

2 frozen underripe bananas

6 tablespoons pure maple syrup

1   Pour the almond milk into a blender.

2   Slice the bananas and add them to the blender along with the maple syrup. Blend until smooth.

Coconut Almond

I love the almond flavor that comes through in this smoothie, as well as the faint hint of coconut. This is a flavor match made in heaven. And my kids agree, judging by how fast they drank this one down!

MAKES 4 (8-OUNCE) SERVINGS

2 cups coconut milk beverage (see page 14)

4 pitted dates

¼ cup almond butter

1 tablespoon agave syrup or honey

2 cups ice cubes

1 Pour the coconut milk into a blender. Add the dates and let them soak in the coconut milk for 10 minutes.

2 Add the almond butter, sweetener, and ice and blend until smooth.

Eggnog

I am obsessed with all things eggnog when the holidays come around. We all know that the traditional drink isn't a health drink, so why not give your kids this good-for-you version? If the taste of the rum extract is too strong for your kids, feel free to leave it out—the smoothie will still be amazing—but I love the authentic eggnog flavor it brings.

MAKES 4 (7-OUNCE) SERVINGS

2 cups almond milk

4 pitted dates

2 frozen underripe bananas

¼ teaspoon freshly grated nutmeg

¼ teaspoon rum extract

1   Pour the almond milk into a blender. Add the dates and let them soak in the almond milk for 10 minutes.

2   Slice the bananas and add them to the blender. Add the nutmeg and rum extract and blend until smooth.

Grape Slush

I had one of those "duh" moments when I came up with this smoothie. We love to snack on frozen grapes, and one day as I was looking at a bag of them in my freezer I suddenly realized how perfectly they would work as the "ice" in a smoothie. This was a total hit with my kids. Abbi thought this smoothie tasted just like a grape popsicle.

MAKES 4 (8-OUNCE) SERVINGS

1½ cups Concord grape juice

2¼ cups frozen red or green seedless grapes

1   Combine the grape juice and grapes in a blender.

2   Blend until smooth.

Bedtime Smoothies

With young children, bedtime is often a struggle. In fact, I dread it pretty much every night. One thing that helps bedtime to go a little more smoothly is to have a bedtime routine. If we skip the routine, things often go haywire.

Because we eat dinner so early, I started adding in a nightly smoothie for my kids as part of the bedtime routine. It filled their bellies so that they could sleep well all night. I started to find out about all kinds of ingredients that have been known to help sleep; for instance, milk contains tryptophan, which helps to make the kids sleepy; bananas are filled with magnesium and potassium, which are both muscle relaxants. I noticed an immediate difference when I started giving my kids a smoothie before bed. Bedtime is still not my favorite time, but the bedtime smoothie sure does help the kids sleep better!

Chamomile Berry

Chamomile tea is believed to have a calming effect. Its flavor is very mild, compared to the flavor of many other herbal teas, and that makes it a great addition to this bedtime smoothie.

MAKES 4 (8-OUNCE) SERVINGS

2 cups brewed chamomile tea, cooled
2 cups mixed frozen berries
1 cup plain Greek yogurt
2 teaspoons agave syrup or honey

1   Pour the cooled chamomile tea into a blender.

2   Add the berries, yogurt, and sweetener and blend until smooth.

Bedtime Cherry

Cherries naturally contain melatonin, which helps regulate sleep and wake cycles. If you can find tart cherries, use them, because they contain the most melatonin. But if you use them you may need to add a little agave syrup as a sweetener.

MAKES 4 (8-OUNCE) SERVINGS

2 cups milk

2 cups frozen cherries

½ teaspoon vanilla extract

1   Pour the milk into a blender.

2   Add the cherries and vanilla extract. Blend until smooth.

Choosing Milk for Smoothies

When a recipe calls for milk, keep the dietary needs and preferences of your children in mind. Because my kids don't have any allergies or restrictions, I stick with cow's milk, but rice, soy, almond, and coconut milk are all options. Different milks might change the overall flavor of a smoothie, so experiment to see if making a substitution will work.

Cinnamon Apple Oatmeal

Oatmeal is loaded with calcium, magnesium, phosphorus, and potassium—all sleep-inducing nutrients. Plus, it also contains melatonin and is a great complex carbohydrate. This is a great smoothie that will fill your kids up so that they won't wake up too hungry in the morning.

MAKES 4 (6-OUNCE) SERVINGS

¾ cup milk

¾ cup apple juice

½ cup old-fashioned oats

1 tablespoon agave syrup, honey, or pure maple syrup

¼ teaspoon ground cinnamon

2 cups ice cubes

1   Pour the milk and apple juice into a blender.

2   Add the oats, sweetener, and cinnamon. Top with the ice and blend until smooth.

Banana Cream

Many people swear by a glass of warm milk to help them sleep. Milk contains tryptophan, an amino acid (also found in turkey) that can make you sleepy. Combine milk with bananas, which contain magnesium and potassium—both natural muscle relaxants—and you have the perfect bedtime smoothie.

MAKES 4 (8-OUNCE) SERVINGS

2 cups milk

2 frozen ripe bananas

1 teaspoon vanilla extract

1 Pour the milk into a blender.

2 Slice the bananas and add them to the blender along with the vanilla. Blend until smooth.

Sleepytime Honey Almond

Almonds are full of not only protein but also magnesium, which is a natural muscle relaxant. This smoothie features almonds in the almond milk as well as in the almond butter, giving the kids a nice dose of magnesium.

MAKES 4 (8-OUNCE) SERVINGS

2 cups almond milk

¼ cup almond butter

¼ cup honey

1 cup ice cubes

1   Pour the almond milk into a blender.

2   Add the almond butter and honey. Top with the ice and blend until smooth.

Peanut Butter & Apple

This is an ideal bedtime smoothie. The peanut butter improves seratonin levels, contributing to feelings of happiness and well-being; the apples contain complex carbohydrates, which keep bellies feeling full longer and will help your children sleep soundly.

MAKES 4 (9-OUNCE) SERVINGS

1 cup milk

1 large or 2 small apples

¼ cup natural peanut butter

2 cups ice cubes

1. Pour the milk into a blender. Core the apple, cut it into chunks, and add it to the blender.

2. Add the peanut butter. Top with the ice and blend until smooth.

Acknowledgments

Thank you to my husband, Josh, for supporting me through the craziness of another cookbook. I know that it often meant a dirty house, crazy kids, and sandwiches for dinner. Thanks for sticking with me through it.

I never could have written this book without my kids, Abbi, Easton, and Camden. Thank you for taste testing every single version of every smoothie in this book. Thank you for your honest feedback and for trying again even if you didn't like something the first time!

Thank you to the whole team at the Harvard Common Press for believing in me. I've said it before, but I never realized just how much goes into producing a cookbook, and I feel like I've had the best team on my side. Thank you for walking me through every step and for making me appreciate all that goes into a print book.

Thank you, thank you, thank you to the readers of Taste and Tell. I still pinch myself knowing that this blog is my job. Thank you for supporting me and for reading my posts all of these years. Thank you for making the recipes on my blog and for your comments and your love. I wouldn't be where I am today without all of the support from my readers. Thank you for making my dreams a reality.

And thank you to my mom for always being the best example of a mom in the kitchen. Thank you for cooking for us kids and for passing on your love of cooking. I only hope to be that kind of example to my kids!

Measurement Equivalents

Please note that all conversions are approximate.

Liquid Conversions

U.S.	Metric
1 tsp	5 ml
1 tbs	15 ml
2 tbs	30 ml
3 tbs	45 ml
¼ cup	60 ml
⅓ cup	75 ml
⅓ cup + 1 tbs	90 ml
⅓ cup + 2 tbs	100 ml
½ cup	120 ml
⅔ cup	150 ml
¾ cup	180 ml
¾ cup + 2 tbs	200 ml
1 cup	240 ml
1 cup + 2 tbs	275 ml
1¼ cups	300 ml
1⅓ cups	325 ml
1½ cups	350 ml
1⅔ cups	375 ml
1¾ cups	400 ml
1¾ cups + 2 tbs	450 ml
2 cups (1 pint)	475 ml
2½ cups	600 ml
3 cups	720 ml
4 cups (1 quart)	945 ml
(1,000 ml is 1 liter)	

Weight Conversions

U.S./U.K.	Metric
½ oz	14 g
1 oz	28 g
1½ oz	43 g
2 oz	57 g
2½ oz	71 g
3 oz	85 g
3½ oz	100 g
4 oz	113 g
5 oz	142 g
6 oz	170 g
7 oz	200 g
8 oz	227 g
9 oz	255 g
10 oz	284 g
11 oz	312 g
12 oz	340 g
13 oz	368 g
14 oz	400 g
15 oz	425 g
1 lb	454 g

Oven Temperature Conversions

°F	Gas Mark	°C
250	½	120
275	1	140
300	2	150
325	3	165
350	4	180
375	5	190
400	6	200
425	7	220
450	8	230
475	9	240
500	10	260
550	Broil	290

Index

Page references in *italics* indicate photographs.

About the Author

 Deborah Harroun's blog, Taste and Tell, has attracted a large and loyal following since she launched it in 2007. In it she writes about family-friendly food, with an emphasis on ease of preparation, good nutrition, and recipes that both kids and parents will enjoy. She is the author of *Red Velvet Lover's Cookbook* (The Harvard Common Press, 2014). Her recipes and writing have been featured or excerpted in numerous other places in print and online, including *Every Day with Rachael Ray, Bon Appétit, Better Homes and Gardens,* iVillage, Babble, The Kitchn, and the Huffington Post. She lives with her husband and three young children in the Salt Lake City area, where she appears frequently as a cooking authority on local television news and lifestyle shows.